Cambridge English Readers

Level 5

Series editor: Philip Prowse

Death in the Dojo

Sue Leather

T0094900

CAMBRIDGE
UNIVERSITY PRESS

CAMBRIDGE
UNIVERSITY PRESS

University Printing House, Cambridge CB2 8BS, United Kingdom

One Liberty Plaza, 20th Floor, New York, NY 10006, USA

477 Williamstown Road, Port Melbourne, VIC 3207, Australia

314–321, 3rd Floor, Plot 3, Splendor Forum, Jasola District Centre, New Delhi – 110025, India

79 Anson Road, #06–04/06, Singapore 079906

Cambridge University Press is part of the University of Cambridge.

It furthers the University's mission by disseminating knowledge in the pursuit of education, learning and research at the highest international levels of excellence.

www.cambridge.org
Information on this title: www.cambridge.org/9780521656214

© Cambridge University Press 1999

First published 1999

Printed in Great Britain by Ashford Colour Press Ltd.

A catalogue record for this publication is available from the British Library

ISBN 978-0-521-65621-4 Paperback

No character in this work is based on any person living or dead. Any resemblance to an actual person or situation is purely accidental.

Contents

Characters

Kate Jensen: a news reporter on The Daily Echo, a national newspaper published in London. She's in her early thirties. She used to train in karate.

Tony Jensen: Kate's eighty-year-old father. He used to be a boxer and also a journalist.

Dave Balzano: Kate's boss. The editor of The Daily Echo.

Rick: Kate's colleague, also a reporter on The Daily Echo.

Jonty Adams: a police contact at Scotland Yard.

Sanjay: An old friend of Kate's from her karate days. He still trains in karate in the Asano dojo in London.

Kawaguchi-sensei: a famous karate teacher and owner of the Zanshin dojo in London.

Jun Kawaguchi: Kawaguchi's son. He lives in London with his wife and children and works for a Japanese bank.

Naoko Kawaguchi: Kawaguchi's daughter. A writer and translator, she now lives in Tokyo, Japan.

Brendan Murphy: Murphy was accused of The London Road murder, over thirty years ago.

Tim: Kate's neighbour.

Glossary

Karate: Karate-do is a Japanese martial art. It means 'the way of the empty hand'. In other words, no weapons are used. There are numerous types of punches and kicks. The training is very hard and is both physical and mental. Students of karate wear a white gi, or karate suit and a belt which shows how long they have been training.

Dojo: means 'the place of the way'. The place where students of karate train.

[1] **Sensei:** teacher, literally 'leader along the way'. Teachers of the martial arts are called 'sensei' by their students.

[2] **Scotland Yard:** the main office of the London police force.

[3] **Black belt:** a high grade in martial arts.

[4] **Gi:** karate suit. Made of thick white cotton. The full name is do-gi, 'suit of the way'.

[5] **Dan:** means 'step'. 1st dan is the lowest grade of black belt, 10th dan is the highest.

[6] **Grade:** level or step.

[7] **Karateka**: karate expert.

[8] **Budo**: means 'the way of war'. Includes all the martial arts – judo, tae-kwondo, ju-jitsu, kendo etc.

[9] **Samurai**: a traditional Japanese soldier.

[10] **Kimono**: traditional Japanese dress.

[11] **Origami**: the Japanese art of paper folding.

[12] **Hai**: 'yes'.

[13] **Sushi**: Japanese food. Usually rice and seafood or vegetables.

[14] **Moshi moshi**: 'hello' (only used when speaking on the telephone).

[15] **Budoka**: martial artist.

[16] **Kiai**: the shout or cry used in karate, particularly when attacking.

Chapter 1 *Death of a fighter*

'You kill the guy with a karate punch to the left kidney. Yaku zuki – reverse punch. You step over the body lying on the wooden floor, take one last look at the face, eyes still open in an expression of surprise, and move quickly through the door of the dojo to the lift. Then down and into the cold night air. You almost allow yourself to smile as you walk towards the Underground station, your right hand still aware of the contact with Kawaguchi-sensei's body. Then you get a train to safety.'

'Cut the poetry, Jensen. This is a newspaper for the twenty-first century – we want facts, not fantasy.' This was the sweet voice of my boss, Dave Balzano, editor of The Daily Echo, as he looked over my shoulder at my computer screen.

'Yes, sir,' I said under my breath as he moved on towards his office. Balzano was a fat, sweaty man with a bad temper. I had learnt from bitter experience that there was no point in arguing with him. I looked again at what I had written.

'Pity,' I whispered to my colleague, Rick. 'I quite like it.' Rick smiled but carried on looking at his screen.

Rick and I were both news reporters on The Daily Echo. I had been working there for about three years and Rick joined about a year after me. Like me, he had started off on a less well-known newspaper outside London, in a small town in Scotland to be exact. All we wrote about were new babies and marriages. I studied journalism in Manchester and, after finishing my studies, got a job with the Manchester Evening News. That was a bit more exciting, but not much.

We had now finally arrived in the big city and we both enjoyed our work.

We were working in The Daily Echo main office on Malvern Street in central London. Our desks were side by side. The only real problem with the job was Dave Balzano. He was a great editor but he had the worst temper in the world. In the three years I had been at The Daily Echo I'd never heard him talk quietly.

'Jensen!! Get the latest news from Scotland Yard and get down to that damn karate place and get an inside story!' shouted Balzano loudly as he went into his office. I smiled sweetly but under my breath I said 'go to hell'.

* * *

I thought over what I knew about Kawaguchi, or Kawaguchi-sensei[1] as he was known to his pupils. I first knew of him some years ago when I trained with Asano-sensei. They had both trained in Tokyo with the great master, Ohtsuka, and had both left Japan at about the same time, in the early 1960s. They were two of a number of teachers who brought the teachings of karate from Japan to Europe at that time. Some years later they had had a very public disagreement about technique and had started rival karate schools. In London, anybody who wanted to train seriously trained with one of them. Now Kawaguchi was lying dead in the Central Hospital, killed by a single punch.

With Balzano's voice still ringing in my ears, I arranged to meet Jonty Adams, my contact at Scotland Yard,[2] in a bar in Piccadilly, our usual meeting place. A reporter's relationship to the police is never an easy one. We need them and they need us. Sometimes, though, getting any useful information out of them was nearly impossible. I was lucky that Jonty Adams liked me. He liked me and I needed him. Perfect.

Jonty was a slim, nervous guy in his late thirties with a thin moustache and terrible taste in ties. He was wearing a particularly horrible grey one with little pink pigs all over it. I tried to ignore it. It wasn't easy.

'So what's happening with the Kawaguchi case?' I asked, trying to be casual, not to make it sound that I was desperate.

'Not much progress on motive, Kate,' he said. He always moved his body a lot when he got excited and the pigs on his tie started to dance around in front of my eyes. 'Though I suppose a guy like that might have a few enemies. You know, probably punched a few people in his time. This I will say though, whoever killed him was a real karate expert. The post mortem showed there'd been just one punch, but of such a force that it killed him immediately.'

I groaned to myself. Jonty had a way of spending a long time repeating things you already knew.

'Obviously the place to look is in the karate clubs,' he went on. Christ! How did these guys get to be in the police? Then, just as I was about to go, he said:

'We took a guy called Ito in for questioning, Kawaguchi's number two – he told us that Kawaguchi had been threatened before.'

'Thank you, God,' I said to myself. I left Jonty and his tie in the bar.

I went over to the Asano dojo for the last half hour of training and saw a good fight among about six black belts.[3] I stood and watched the white gi's[4] moving quickly round the wooden floor, black belts flying. There was something beautiful about this, more like a dance rather than a fight. It made me feel sad, not to be there doing it. One of the black belts was my friend, Sanjay. While he was having a shower I went over to the Red Cow pub just behind the training hall on Clapham Common, ordered a couple of beers and waited for him. I was glad to see him; Sanjay and I had been friends for years. We started training together and took our dan[5] grades[6] together too. We were more like brother and sister than just friends.

Sanjay was a small delicate Indian man of about twenty-six, with the most beautiful dark eyes and long eyelashes. He came from a southern Indian family who now lived near Birmingham. His father was a surgeon in a big teaching hospital and Sanjay also qualified as a doctor two years ago. He was a gentle, charming man. You couldn't imagine him hurting a fly, but he fought like a tiger. 'The Indian tiger', I called him. We took our beers and sat in the public bar.

'Nobody can believe that Kawaguchi is dead. It seems incredible,' said Sanjay, drinking his beer thirstily.

'How many people do you think would be capable of that – killing someone with one blow to the kidney?' I asked.

'Quite a few unfortunately. Any of those guys tonight could have done it if they'd timed the punch right. There must be a hundred guys in London like that. Even I could have done it – even you, Kate!' Sanjay smiled. 'The question is, why didn't Kawaguchi stop him? He was supposed to be one of the greatest fighters ever.'

Yes, my old friend, I thought. That was exactly the question. How did some guy – if it was a man – manage to catch Kawaguchi before the great man could defend himself? Kawaguchi was known as "the cat" and was said to be so fast that in practice he would hit you as soon as you thought of moving. These old masters got faster as they got older.

'Yes, it's a real mystery,' Sanjay continued, thoughtfully. 'And what about you Kate, are you doing any training?' Sanjay asked the same question every time I saw him and he always got the same answer.

'No, Sanjay, no real training. I just try to keep fit, you know. A bit of swimming.'

I had trained for about ten years in all, but a number of injuries and a doctor's warning had persuaded me to give up. I missed it a lot, particularly when I was with Sanjay. He reminded me of the companionship I no longer had.

We chatted about our karate friends for a while and drank another couple of beers. At about 10.45 we left the pub and walked towards the Underground together. The night was cold and uninviting after the warmth of the pub. Autumn was beginning to turn into winter.

'Goodnight Kate,' said Sanjay. 'Why don't you come to practice some time? You're getting lazy.'

Dear Sanjay, he never gave up. I suppose that's what made him such a great fighter. He smiled his slow friendly smile as we parted to take different trains home.

28th September 1960
Brixton Prison

Dear Mum and Dad

Thank you so much for coming to see me yesterday. It made me feel a lot better, I can tell you. And thank you for having faith in me – it means a lot to me in these difficult times. You don't realise how much you need your family until you're in this kind of mess.

My solicitor, Mr Jeffreys, came today and we had a good chat. I felt much better after that. He's a very intelligent man and he is doing his best for me. I feel that there are people on my side, people like him who know that I am innocent of this terrible crime. I think it can only be a matter of time before they realise what an awful mistake they've made!

I couldn't believe it when that girl picked me out of the identity parade. I've never seen her before in my life!! It's a terrible mistake and sooner or later they'll realise it. In a way I am looking forward to the trial so that we can prove the truth of this once and for all.

Anyway, enough of all that. I hope you are well and that Paddy and Ian are fine. Tell Ian that I'll take him to the football again when I get out of here. I miss you all very much.

God bless

Brendan

Chapter 2   *Death follows death*

Back home in my sixth floor Brixton flat I turned the lights down low and listened to the guy who lived upstairs, Tim, playing the saxophone. He was playing a Ben Webster tune, one of my favourites. The long notes of the sax came through the ceiling. I was in the mood for jazz, as usual. I lay back on my sofa and looked out of the window – London by night, the sweetest sight in the whole world. It was a clear, bright October evening and I took in a view that stretched from the dark streets of Brixton to Docklands.

Brixton was not the best area of London to live in. For me, though, there were some very good reasons for living there. First of all, it was a lot cheaper than some other places in the city. I also had my own private saxophonist living upstairs and this fantastic view over London. What more did I need?

I looked now at that view. The sky was deep blue and the stars looked like tiny jewels all over it. The moon would be full in a few days and it was already big and beautiful. I let the music wash over me. The tune coming from upstairs was sad, full of lost dreams and lost love. I thought about Kawaguchi, dying so far away from his real home and I suddenly felt bad. I took the "Who's Who in the Martial Arts" off the bookshelf and opened it at Kawaguchi. It read:

Kawaguchi, Takehiko, 8th Dan, born 1925, Osaka, Japan. Student of the great Ohtsuka, 10th Dan, Japan National Team 1950–58. World Champion fighter 1954–56. Started Zanshin School of Karate, London, 1960.

Not much there. Not much for a whole lifetime. I decided to get some sleep. Tomorrow I would have to go to the Zanshin dojo and I was going to need all my strength.

I went to bed and dreamt that I was in the dojo again, with Sanjay. We were fighting but we were both smiling. I was woken by a loud ringing noise next to my left ear. It felt like it was the middle of the night. I came back to life, realised it was the phone and picked it up. It was Jonty.

'What do you want? What time is it?' I asked crossly, reaching for my watch on the bedside table.

'Get down to the Kawaguchi training hall, Kate. We've found another body.'

By the time I got to Waterloo Station it was 6.30 am. I had some difficulty keeping my eyes open. I had planned to go to the Zanshin dojo today, but not quite this early. I ran from the station to the dojo, a few minutes away. It was already busy down there. The shape of a man was drawn on the changing-room floor and there were a lot of police. Only a couple of reporters though. Rampton from The Standard newspaper and some new guy from The Observer. Jonty, wearing a purple tie with yellow flowers, was smoking nervously.

'Same story,' Jonty said through the smoke. 'Looks like one punch – to the stomach this time – right on the solar plexus. No sign of a struggle. The guy had just showered and changed after a training session. The cleaner found him this morning. It was Ito, Kawaguchi's number two. We're telling the rest of the club to stay at home and closing the dojo for the moment.'

The Zanshin dojo had not only lost its sensei, Kawaguchi, but now Ito was also gone. I wondered what effect it would have on the dojo, on the students. I turned my cassette recorder on and did a brief two-minute description of the scene. I kept to the facts. Balzano is keen on facts.

A punch to the solar plexus could be deadly and on this occasion it had been. I had once seen someone hit like that in a competition. He fell to the floor, unable to get up; they had to carry him off. He didn't die, of course, because his opponent wasn't using full force. Hiromitsu Ito hadn't been so lucky. It must have happened about the time I met Sanjay last night. While we were sitting in the pub having a beer, somebody waited until everyone had gone, went into the training hall, then into the changing room and killed yet another top fighter with one punch.

3rd October 1960
Brixton Prison

Dear Paddy

Well, little brother, I hope that you are looking after Mum and Dad properly while I am not around. You're the eldest now – at least until I get home.

Things are all right here. They are treating me pretty well under the circumstances. The prison officers are OK – we manage to have a laugh and joke together. It's not like home though! I just keep hoping that if I carry on telling the truth, telling everyone that I didn't do it, someone will believe me.

The only thing keeping me going at the moment is the fact that I've got my solicitor, Mr Jeffreys and my barrister, Mr Johnston on my side. Mr Johnston's the one that's going to deal with my case at the trial. That starts next week and I don't mind telling you that I'll be happy when it starts. At least I'll have a chance to tell everyone the truth, that I was in Manchester that day.

Look after yourself, Paddy, and look after Mum and Dad and Ian. When I get out of here, we'll go and have a drink or two together like we used to.

Love

Brendan

Chapter 3   *Like fathers ...*

Jun Kawaguchi opened the door of his Wimbledon home. He was a slim, reserved man of about thirty, who even in his obvious sadness for his dead father, remembered how to be polite to guests. I had been surprised that he had agreed to see me and I said so to him.

'I often read your articles, Miss Jensen. You understand karate. You understand many things,' Jun replied.

I liked this man. He seemed to have good taste.

'My father was a very popular man, as I am sure you know, Miss Jensen,' he went on. 'He was well respected by everybody he met.'

It was true. I had seen Kawaguchi-sensei give a demonstration about five years ago at Crystal Palace. He was a great karateka.[7] He was also a quiet, gentle man, as polite as his son. It was hard to believe he was a man with enemies.

'Can you think of anyone who hated him or disliked him?' I asked.

'The police asked me that. Well, you know of course that he and Asano-sensei had a big argument about twenty years ago and they never spoke again, as far as I know. I don't think they really hated each other though; it was a matter of principle more than anything. Anyway, Asano died last year as you know.'

I had written about his death in The Daily Echo.

Asano-sensei had died of throat cancer after a very long illness. The matter of principle that Jun talked about was about a number of techniques. Kawaguchi claimed that Asano was moving too far away from the teachings of their master, Ohtsuka-sensei. Asano, for his part, felt that he was making progress. In the end they had a huge argument and never spoke to each other again. These guys got excited about things like that.

'I don't know of any other enemies,' he said, 'my father was a peaceful man, like all great masters.'

It was true that the great masters seemed to have an unusual sense of peace around them. I had once met Ohtsuka-sensei, in Japan, two years before he died; he had been training for about fifty years by that time. He was a kind, smiling man with no sense of aggression about him. His face seemed to shine with a kind of peace. That was perhaps the most attractive thing about martial arts training: how training in the arts of war – or budo[8] as it is called in Japanese – could make you less, not more, aggressive.

Jun asked me to excuse him and went out of the room to make some tea.

I looked around the sitting room of the comfortable home. There were signs of children – toys in the corner and pictures of the family on top of the piano. Jun and his wife with a little boy of about eight and a girl of about five. Formal-looking photographs including one of Jun's father, severe-faced, in traditional Japanese dress with a samurai[9] sword by his side. Apart from that, there were few signs of Japan, just an old print of a Japanese lady in a kimono[10] on the wall and a few origami[11] birds that the kids had probably made.

I was looking at the tiny coloured paper birds when Jun came back into the room with a tray.

'They're cranes,' said Jun. 'In Japan they symbolise good fortune. They don't seem to have brought my family any good fortune though, do they Miss Jensen?'

I didn't answer but accepted a cup of Japanese green tea which Jun gave to me with both hands, in the traditional Japanese manner. The slightly bitter taste of the tea was strangely comforting.

Then Jun said, 'The children are at school. My wife has gone to look after my mother. She is very upset, as you can imagine.' Jun's face became very serious, almost solemn, and for a moment he looked just like his father in the formal samurai photograph. 'I am making the arrangements for my father's funeral.'

'Why did your family leave Japan?' I asked.

'My father was one of the chosen few who came to Europe to teach karate-do. He believed it was his fate, it was what he had to do. He started training when he was nine years old, he knew nothing else. It was his life. He chose Britain because he had learnt English at university and spent a year in London. He liked it. He had friends here.'

'Do you study karate yourself?' I asked.

'I did, until about five years ago,' Jun replied. 'It was hard not to follow my father when I was a child. I am the only son you know. But now I work in the city for a Japanese bank and I am a family man, as you can see.' He nodded his head in the direction of the photograph of his wife and two children. 'Anyway, I could never be as good as my father. It's hard, you understand.'

Yes, I did. I understood exactly.

My dad grew up in the East End, the poor part of London. They say there are only two ways out of the East End; one is to become a criminal, the other is to become a boxer. Dad chose boxing. As a young man he was a professional boxer. Even though he was now eighty, he still moved like a boxer, and looked like one. He had had his nose broken twice. He had had a promising career in the boxing ring but the Second World War interrupted it. He ended up wandering around Italy in hiding from the Germans. He learnt Italian but lost his career. When he got back to London after the end of the war it was too late for him to carry on boxing; he had lost five years. He had an old friend who worked for a news agency – he helped Dad and Dad became a journalist.

As a child I remember the phone ringing constantly at home. Dad was always on a story and rushing around madly. My mother was the calm one. It was my Dad who taught me how to fight. He never treated me any differently from my brother. He showed me how to fight with my fists up when I was five and to get up quickly if I fell down. I was never allowed to give up. When my brother and I fought and I fell down he would count ... '10, 9, 8, 7 ...' as if he were the referee at a boxing match. I always got up before he counted down. It was a lesson that would be useful to me many times over the years. Whenever something bad happens in my life and I feel like giving up, I hear Dad's voice in my ears, telling me to get up off the floor.

When I was nine he gave me a punch bag as a birthday present. I remember telling my teachers at school about it, assuming that they would be as happy as I was. They were shocked, I think, as was my mother, but I was so proud of that punch bag. Dad hung it up for me in the playroom and after school I would go and practise punches for hours. I still have it, though it is now old and soft.

I suppose it was natural that I would end up being interested in the martial arts, though for me it was karate, not boxing. We were always arguing about which was the best fighting system, boxing or karate. We were both certain that we were right, of course. Dad would still spend hours showing me boxing techniques in his living room, as he had when I was a kid.

'Look,' he would say, demonstrating his favourite punch, the right hook. 'What punch can be more effective than that?' I am sure that it had been deadly in its day. But he was – is – the sweetest person in the world and even as a young man, was never aggressive, except in the boxing ring. I suppose he was the one who taught me that you can be a fighter and be peace-loving at the same time.

I also became a journalist of course, just like him. I was following in Dad's footsteps – and it wasn't always easy. Dad read The Daily Echo every day and he read my stories with particular interest. He would phone me when I had written something he disagreed with, or when he thought my style was not quite right. Sometimes I would get cross, but more often than not he was right.

Later that day I was at his home in Chiswick. He had had a bath and, with a towel round his neck, he looked like he had just stepped out of the boxing ring. We chatted about this and that and then I told him about the Kawaguchi murder.

'Kawaguchi. I'm sure I know that name,' he said and scratched his head, trying to remember from where and when. This could have taken a long time. I was never sure whether Dad's memory was bad because he was old, or because he'd been hit in the head so many times when he was in the boxing ring. I sometimes thought it was a mixture of both.

'He was pretty famous,' I offered.

'Yes ... but I'm sure ... there's something ...' He tried to get his memory to work, with no success. Eventually, he gave up. We talked of other things and forgot about it.

When I got home that evening there were two messages on my answerphone. One was from Balzano: 'Where the hell are you? And what's happening on those Japanese murders?' The other was Dad: 'I've remembered what it was ... Kawaguchi ... that was the name of the girl who was involved in the London Road case when John Blakeston was murdered. I've got some newspaper cuttings here.'

10th October 1960
Brixton Prison

Darling Janey

Thank you for coming to see me yesterday. I'm sorry that I was feeling a bit down after the first few days of the trial. It is very hard for me, you know, being accused of this horrible crime and knowing that I didn't do it, that I am innocent. Sometimes I feel like I'm in a nightmare and any minute I'm going to wake up and it'll be all over.

There are all kinds of lies being said at the trial, and I just have to sit and listen to it, for the most part. I can't wait until it is my turn to speak – then I will really show them. I only have to prove that I was in Manchester and nowhere near where they say I was.

Anyway, I am sure that this thing will be all over soon. I was quite surprised by what you told me yesterday. I won't talk about it now, for obvious reasons.* But you must have faith that everything will be all right in the end. And you know that I could never have committed an awful crime like this, don't you?

Please pray for me, darling Janey, lovely Lovat.

Love

Brendan

* Letters from prison would be checked and read by prison officers.

Chapter 4   *The past*

Next morning I went back to Dad's to have a look at the newspaper cuttings on the London Road case. On the Underground between Brixton and Chiswick I thought over what I knew about it. I was only a baby when it happened but later I heard about it from both my parents. It was the most famous murder of its time and Dad had been very involved in it. In fact, he was one of the first journalists to write about the story in the national press, mainly because he had a good contact in the police.

A young school caretaker called Blakeston had taken a sixteen-year-old schoolgirl home from a private school in Surrey. She had fainted and wasn't feeling well. The drive to her home went through the countryside down the London Road. A man had hitched a lift, saying that his car had broken down and he needed to get to London. After a few miles, the man took out a gun and made Blakeston drive around the countryside for hours. After about four or five hours, he made Blakeston stop the car. By this time it was dark and they were in the middle of nowhere.

According to the girl, he had promised them he wouldn't shoot them. But Blakeston made an unexpected move and the gunman shot him. Blakeston died instantly. The man had shot him through the head. The girl, not surprisingly, panicked; she opened the car door and ran. She was shot three times in the back as she was running away. Incredibly, the girl survived, though she never walked again. A farmer found Blakeston's body and the girl next morning. She was able to describe the murderer to the police of course. Kawaguchi's daughter was still alive somewhere, I remembered, in a wheelchair. I thought about Jun and his comment about the birds of good fortune: a sister in a wheelchair and a murdered father hardly seemed like good luck.

At Dad's house, I looked through the old newspaper cuttings, a huge pile of them, all kept in an old file in his study. Everything was there, from the finding of the body, then the public anger and the search for the murderer, to the hanging. Then I saw:

Murphy – the London Road murderer. Sixteen-year-old Naoko Kawaguchi identified Brendan Murphy of Islington, North London, as the London Road murderer in an identity parade today.

'Naoko Kawaguchi picked out Murphy at an identity parade,' said Dad, 'even though she had first said that the murderer had black hair. Murphy had light brown hair. It was obvious the girl was very upset. She didn't know what she was saying. There was no motive either. Even the prosecution never suggested a motive. The girl wasn't raped. Murphy was a burglar and a car thief. He had never committed a violent crime. He didn't know either Blakeston or the Kawaguchi girl. The whole thing was unbelievable.'

Then there were a lot of newspaper cuttings about the trial, many of them written by Dad. It was obvious that by this time Dad was convinced that Murphy was innocent. A lot of other people, many of them politicians and civil rights campaigners, became involved in the campaign to save Murphy. There were desperate appeals from his family – he came from a large Irish family settled in north London. But no-one was able to save him and he was finally hanged, in February 1961. One of the last people to be hanged in Britain. There were pictures of a good-looking young man with light brown hair and pale skin. He didn't look like a murderer, but then I suppose no-one ever did.

'The campaign went on after his death and a lot of famous people got involved – politicians, lawyers and journalists,' Dad explained. 'We wanted to clear his name and also to get the government to stop hanging people. It was stopped eventually, but it was too late for poor Brendan Murphy. There was a public enquiry some years later, but the whole thing was a joke.'

'A joke? You mean someone was trying to hide something?' I asked.

'I think the government realised that they had made a mistake and of course they tried to cover it up. They'd hanged someone for it, the public was satisfied – why bring it all up again?' Dad replied.

'Can you remember anything about the girl's parents?' I asked.

'Not much. Except that they wanted revenge. The whole thing was so awful that a lot of people just wanted revenge for it. I think they felt that justice had been done. Wait … I'm sure there's an article there in which they mention something about the girl's father.'

I looked through the pile of newspaper cuttings and found a picture of Kawaguchi looking young. He was wearing a dark suit and tie. He looked very like Jun. I then read the article below the picture:

Mr Kawaguchi, the girl's father and a famous teacher of the martial art of karate said that he was satisfied that Blakeston's murderer had been found and punished. He felt that, though it would not bring Blakeston back, or make his daughter walk again, it was right that Murphy should be hanged.

That was about all there was on the family.

'I only met Kawaguchi once. He seemed very cold, very distant,' said Dad. 'I remember trying to tell him that I thought Murphy was not the murderer, that Murphy was innocent. That we were hanging an innocent man. But he didn't listen. Something strange happens to people in these situations.'

'Is there any possibility that Murphy did do it?' I asked.

Dad shook his head. 'No, I don't think so. Not in my opinion – there was no motive, no history of that kind of crime … And then he had an alibi showing that he was somewhere else at the time of the killing. He was almost certainly in Manchester at the time the murder was committed, trying to sell some stolen jewellery. Here, read this.'

Dad threw me a paperback book called "Who Killed Murphy?" written by a famous journalist, Julia Redmond. I went home, wondering if this thirty-year-old story had any connection with the recent murders.

20th October 1960
Brixton Prison

Dear Mum and Dad

I can't tell you how disappointed I am after being in the witness stand today. It seems that everyone is determined not to believe me and no-one is prepared to stand up for me. I could see you sitting there and it gave me strength; it was the only thing that kept me going I can tell you. Sometimes it's hard to keep cheerful, in the face of all these lies.

I know that Mr Jeffreys and Mr Johnson are doing their very best for me and I must have faith in them. Once they can find someone who saw I was in Manchester on the day of the murder everything will be fine. I am sure that any day now they will come up with something that will prove my innocence once and for all. It's only a matter of time.

Give my love to Paddy and Ian.

Your loving son

Brendan

Chapter 5 *A bit of a criminal*

The next day I really started work on the Murphy case. I needed to see Paddy Murphy, Brendan's only surviving brother. The youngest Murphy brother, Ian, died in a car accident ten years ago. I found out from The Daily Echo information service that Paddy was now living in Peterborough. On the train I started to read the book Dad had given me about the Murphy case. It made interesting reading. There was a man called Peter Benson who had confessed to the crime after Murphy had been hanged. The authorities didn't take him very seriously because he was slightly crazy and he didn't seem to have a motive either. Or not one they could discover. Anyway, they had already hanged Murphy. There was also a story that Blakeston and the girl were lovers. This had been denied by the girl herself and by her family.

Paddy Murphy was a man of about sixty-five. As he opened the door and showed me into his tiny house, I noticed that he looked like the pictures of Brendan I had seen in the newspapers. The same pale skin and deep brown eyes. His house was small but neat and clean.

'Yes, I know that Kawaguchi's dead. I read it in the newspaper. I'm not sorry,' he said with some feeling. 'He was more responsible than anyone for what happened to Brendan. Kawaguchi was so sure that Brendan did it – God knows why, and he influenced his daughter. She changed her story again and again.'

We talked about Brendan, the elder brother he lost over thirty years ago.

'Brendan was a bit of a criminal – the family have never denied that. He was a car thief and a burglar. He and his friend Johnny West were always breaking into houses here and there. But he wasn't a murderer. There was no way he murdered Blakeston and everybody knew that. He was a young man – he liked girls, cars, having fun. He became a thief so that he could have all those things. But Brendan was no murderer.'

'What do you mean – everybody knew that?' I asked.

'I mean, there was some kind of cover-up, somebody knew, somebody knows who did it. A lot of people think it was that guy Benson,' he replied.

'How did your family take it?' I went on.

'They were shocked at first, of course, when he was arrested by the police. They couldn't believe it. But then everybody thought the real murderer would be found eventually, that it was just a matter of time. Anybody who knew Brendan knew that he hadn't done it. And everybody trusted the court. It makes you laugh doesn't it? Then, when he was hanged, it destroyed the family. Completely. My mother died of a broken heart and my father became more and more bitter. He started a campaign to get a pardon from the government. When he realised that he was never going to get it, he took up drinking heavily and died a few years later,' Paddy said.

As I was leaving Paddy Murphy looked at me sadly.

'Leave it alone, girl,' he said. 'A lot of people have tried to find out what really happened and a lot of people have failed. Brendan's gone and nothing will ever bring him back.'

On the train home I stared out of the window at the flat lands around Peterborough and wondered about the cover-up idea. Why had Brendan Murphy been chosen and what was being covered up exactly? Was it just a mistake or was there something more serious behind it all?

Back at the office I spent part of the next day checking the names of all the black belts in the London area. Surprisingly, not one Murphy.

The next morning, the day of Kawaguchi's funeral, I phoned Jun Kawaguchi to ask him about his sister.

'You didn't say anything about the Murphy case and the fact that your sister Naoko was shot by the London Road murderer,' I said.

'I didn't think there was a connection, Miss Jensen. It all happened a long time ago,' Jun replied.

Maybe there was a connection, maybe there wasn't. I was hearing this phrase 'a long time ago' a lot, though, and it was beginning to worry me. In my experience, things that happened a long time ago can have a pretty powerful influence on the present.

'Anyway, I think I should talk to her later,' I said.

'She is not here, Miss Jensen,' Jun replied. He told me that Naoko was not coming to her father's funeral. She was too ill to travel. She lived in Tokyo, a thirteen-hour flight away.

Chapter 6   *The Avenger*

'You want to go where?' screamed Balzano.

'Tokyo,' I repeated.

'Have you gone completely mad, Jensen?' Balzano shouted.

'Listen, I think I'm onto a huge story here,' I said hopefully. I told him what I had got so far. I had to admit that when I put it all together, it didn't sound much. Not many hard, cold facts.

I held my breath and expected the worst but Balzano was in an unusually good mood, because he said:

'Well, all right, Jensen ... but just for three days ... and if you don't get something good out of this, you're in big trouble. And what about Ito – you seem to be forgetting that Ito's been killed too.'

'I don't think this is about Ito. I think Ito was just killed because he knew too much,' I said, hoping that I was right. Balzano looked doubtful but didn't say anything. I phoned the personnel department to get me a ticket to Tokyo and rushed out of the door with my cassette recorder. I had a funeral to go to.

Kawaguchi's funeral was a big affair at a church near the family home; his widow was a Christian. Mrs Kawaguchi, a tiny, thin woman of about sixty-five, was being comforted by Jun and her daughter-in-law. It was much the same as every other funeral I'd been to – an unhappy affair. The only difference was the guests. As well as the family, there were hundreds of karate people from all over the country. Wall-to-wall black suits. I knew many of the faces from the magazine 'Martial Arts Monthly'. Ito's widow wasn't there, though. A pity; I needed to see her before I went to Japan. I wanted to know what Kawaguchi had told Ito. I wanted to know why Ito had been killed. I asked a few people about Ito's wife but nobody was willing to let me know where she was. The karate people were protecting their own kind.

After the funeral, I went into a nearby café for a cup of tea and had a look through the London telephone book. There were ten Itos living in London. I phoned them all and of course she was the last one of the ten I tried. I asked her if we could arrange a meeting.

'No, I don't want to see anyone, Miss Jensen,' said Mrs Ito. 'It's too dangerous – I have children. Please leave us alone.'

I was surprised by the fact that Mrs Ito was not Japanese, but English. A Londoner.

'Please, Mrs Ito, it could save more lives,' I said, and eventually I persuaded her to talk to me on the phone.

'What did Mr Kawaguchi tell your husband?' I asked.

'I'm not sure exactly, but it was something to do with that murder over thirty years ago. He'd received letters, asking him to clear Brendan Murphy's name – for years I think. At first he didn't take it very seriously. The letters became increasingly threatening over the years. He told my husband about most of it – they were very good friends. I don't know how much my husband told the police,' Mrs Ito replied.

'Were all the letters written by the same person?' I went on.

'Yes, I think so,' she said. 'Yes, definitely. It was the same handwriting. The letters were signed "The Avenger". Apparently, they threatened Kawaguchi and his family, almost constantly. In the end they got him – and my husband.' Mrs Ito sighed deeply.

'Do you think Kawaguchi had any idea who "The Avenger" was?' I asked. If Kawaguchi had known who 'The Avenger' was he could have told Ito. That, at least, would be a motive for Ito's murder.

'I don't think so,' she replied. 'I think he just thought it was some madman.'

'Thank you, Mrs Ito, you've been very helpful,' I said. 'I'm sorry to disturb you at this time.'

Then I phoned Jonty. 'Did Kawaguchi ever report these threatening letters to the police?' I asked.

'No, nobody knew anything about them ... except Ito of course,' Jonty answered.

'Where are they now, these letters?' I asked.

'We couldn't find any of them. He must have destroyed them so that his family wouldn't find them,' Jonty said.

So, Kawaguchi had been threatened for years. But by whom? Who was "The Avenger"? And why hadn't Kawaguchi told the police about it?

10th November 1960
Brixton Prison

Dear Johnny

Today I am about as low as I've ever been in my life. I couldn't believe it when the judge gave the verdict – it was like they were talking about somebody else. How can it be that an innocent man is going to be hanged? Of course we're going to appeal against it but right at this moment I don't feel too optimistic.

I want to ask you something as a friend, Johnny. I want you to look after Mum and Dad now and over the next few months. I want you to see that they're OK. It's a terrible shock for them and I worry about them all the time. I know that they're strong, but it would mean a lot to me if you went to see them regularly, just to make sure that they're keeping cheerful.

Johnny, I don't know how it can have happened to me, this thing. I know that you and me have done a few bad things in our time, but you know I could never do something like this. I just keep thinking that I'll wake up one day and it'll all be over, like a bad dream.

All the best, Johnny

Brendan

Chapter 7 *Night caller*

I was going to Tokyo the next day to find Naoko Kawaguchi, so I decided to go straight home after the talk with Mrs Ito. I wanted to listen to some jazz music, relax in a hot bath and have an early night.

As I opened the door of the flat, I reached out my hand to switch on the light. Suddenly I felt an arm swing sharply round my neck from behind, stopping me breathing. Then I felt a knee in the bottom of my back. The force of the knee pushed me into the living room and I fell face down on the floor. The attacker got on top of me and pulled my arm up behind my back so hard that it hurt – a lot. I made an effort not to cry out. I struggled but could hardly move a centimetre. The surprise of the attack made it very effective. I tried to get up but it was no use; I was trapped. The body on top of me was light – it felt like a small man – or a woman – but very strong. Then I felt a sharp pain across the side of my face and I felt like I was falling into water. I couldn't feel anything any more.

I didn't know how long I had been lying there when I woke up. The room was going round and round and I was very cold. I was shaking with cold. I could hear the saxophone upstairs and I crawled on my hands and knees towards the kitchen, where I knew there was a brush. It took a long time; I felt weak. Finally, after what seemed like hours, I managed to reach the brush. I got hold of it and tried to stand up, leaning on the handle. I felt shaky but I managed to push the handle of the brush up towards the living room ceiling and knock. I heard the sax stop but then start again. I knocked again.

'Come on, Tim!' I said under my breath. Then, thankfully, after about five minutes, the sax finally stopped and I heard footsteps coming down towards my flat. I crawled on my knees to the door as he stopped outside and called, 'Kate, are you OK?'

'Tim,' I said weakly, through the closed door, 'wait, I'm just opening it.' I managed, somehow, to get to my feet.

'Christ! What's happened to you?' Tim, who's a big guy, picked me up and carried me towards my bed.

Once I was warm under the bedcovers he said:

'I'd better call the doctor – you've been unconscious.'

'No, don't! It's OK. I'll be fine. I'd rather leave it. Just get me an ice pack,' I replied.

'Whatever you say,' Tim looked worried and went off to the kitchen.

Half an hour later, I was lying there drinking whisky and hot water with an ice pack round the right side of my head, feeling like I might die. I felt so bad that I thought it might be nice to die. I tried to tell Tim what had happened but I was feeling confused and in the end I gave up and just rested.

'I'll sleep here tonight, on the sofa,' said Tim, 'just in case he comes back.'

'Or she,' I said, thinking that Tim would have little chance against whoever it was who attacked me. Still, it was a nice thought. Maybe Sanjay was right, maybe I ought to start training again. Then I fell asleep.

When I woke up next morning, I felt as though I had a hangover from drinking too much. Despite the ice pack, I had a huge blue bruise down one side of my face and it felt swollen and sore.

'Wow!' said Tim sleepily, looking up from the sofa as I walked slowly through the living room on my way to the kitchen for tea. 'You look terrible.'

'You say the sweetest things, Tim,' I replied.

We sat together on the sofa drinking tea. It was a painful business. The hot tea hurt my mouth.

'Lucky my jaw isn't broken,' I said, looking in a hand mirror, 'Looks like it was done with an elbow – the elbow is the hardest bone in the body. Whoever it was obviously didn't mean to do me too much harm.'

'We've got to get those lights fixed outside,' said Tim, shaking his head.

The lights between the lift and the doors on the sixth floor weren't working. This meant that, as you got out of the lift, there was an area of darkness before you got into the flat. Perfect if someone wanted to hide. Perfect for my attacker.

'Who was it, Kate?' asked Tim.

'I didn't get a chance to ask,' I said crossly. Then, 'I don't know, Tim, but I do know that whoever it was, they could have killed me if they'd wanted to. Some damn good technique too – somebody who's been trained, I'm pretty sure.' Even when I was in pain I appreciated good technique. 'It was a warning, though, not an attempt at murder,' I said. But I knew that whoever had hit me could certainly kill someone.

20th December 1960
Brixton Prison

Dear Janey

Thanks for your letter – your letters mean a lot to me, I can tell you. I'm glad you've moved away for a bit. I think that was a good idea. I hope you're well and things are progressing in the right way.

I just sit here thinking about the good times we've had and how nice it would be to be out of this. Once all this is over, I'll make it up to you, I promise. These last few months have made me see life in a totally different way. Now, the only thing I want is to settle down with a nice girl like you and have a family(!) I've learnt my lesson, I can tell you. Life is too short to waste.

Well, it is just a few days before Christmas and I can tell you that prison is not a good place to be at this time. Not very jolly, if you know what I mean. The only thing to look forward to is news of my appeal to the Home Secretary, but I don't think I'll hear anything until after Christmas now.

I'm looking forward to your visit next week. In the meantime, Happy Christmas and look after yourself.

All my love

Brendan

Chapter 8   *Destination Tokyo*

At five o'clock that afternoon I was sitting on the British Airways flight from Heathrow to Tokyo, thinking. It wasn't easy with such an awful headache. Somebody was obviously warning me to stay away from the Murphy case. OK. Let's start with the simple questions. How did they know that I was investigating it? Mmm ... that was already a difficult one. They could have found out from anywhere. If the attacker was a karate person, and it seemed like they were, it could have been at Kawaguchi's funeral. I'd talked to a lot of people and made it clear that I wanted to talk to Mrs Ito. I tried to remember the people at the church but all I could see was just lots of black suits. Perhaps I would think about that later, when I felt better. If I ever did feel better.

I had a sleep, and woke later to find the air hostess offering me something to eat. I ate the cold meat and salad and stared out of the window. Nothing but blackness. We must have been somewhere over Siberia. I decided to try to finish "Who Killed Murphy?" – the book Dad had given me. There were another seven hours to go – plenty of time.

I wondered about this guy Benson. At the time the book was written, the late 1980s, he was living in London. Was he still alive now, I wondered? If so, I would try to find him when I got back from Tokyo. But I would have to start being a bit more careful; whoever was trying to warn me off was pretty serious about it.

We landed at Narita Airport at about two in the afternoon. I wasn't feeling great, what with the aching head and the time difference. The journey from Narita to the centre didn't help. Though not a long journey, it was too much after such a long flight. Tokyo looked very much like I remembered it – busy. It was the kind of city that buzzed twenty-four hours a day. I had been there three years before with my karate club, but we had stayed in a part of the city called Asakusa, and we had trained in a dojo in that area too.

I didn't know the Waseda area, where The Daily Echo's personnel department had booked me into the Hotel Rhiga. Knowing the personnel department as I did, I had expected it would be a cheap hotel in a bad part of town. I was pleasantly surprised to find quite a reasonable hotel in a respectable part of town. Not luxury by Tokyo standards, but OK. Thank you, personnel department.

I went to my room, had a quick shower and changed my clothes. I didn't have much time to waste. I had got Naoko Kawaguchi's address from her brother. He said he would ring her and tell her I was coming. I wondered how she would react to my visit. Jun had not been very happy about me wanting to see his sister, but I found it hard to work out why. Naoko Kawaguchi had returned to Japan twenty years ago. Perhaps they just didn't really know each other or perhaps they didn't get on. Maybe he was upset that she wasn't going back for her father's funeral, though it was hardly her fault if she was ill.

I took a taxi to Miss Kawaguchi's house from the hotel. I have never been able to figure out Japanese addresses and didn't think I would have much of a chance in my present state. Anyway, I love Japanese taxis with their white-gloved drivers and automatic doors. I showed the driver the address and he smiled and said 'hai'[12] in a friendly kind of way. I sat back and relaxed in the back seat and looked out of the window. We drove out through the spreading suburbs of Tokyo through what seemed like a million sets of traffic lights. London had looked grey and rainy when I had left. The Tokyo sky was clear and bright and it was a few degrees warmer than back home. Even my head had stopped aching. It seemed like life might improve.

As we drove through Tokyo I wondered if Naoko Kawaguchi would talk to me, a stranger – and a foreign stranger – about her terrible experience so many years ago. Everything I knew about Japan and the Japanese people told me that it would be difficult for her. I would have to be very careful.

She lived out in the suburbs at Tachikawa in a traditional little house with tatami mats on the floors. Jun had told me that his sister was a writer and translator which meant that she could work from home and from her wheelchair. A tiny, smiling housekeeper came to the door and showed me into the study, with much running around and hands waving. Naoko Kawaguchi was sitting there in her wheelchair. She was surrounded by books and newspapers and on her desk was a computer.

Jun's sister was a middle-aged woman with greying hair who had obviously been pretty once. Now she looked ill and tired, but was as polite as her brother.

'Come in, come in. I've been expecting you,' she said, smiling and moving her wheelchair towards me. 'My brother said you were a journalist looking into my father's death, Miss Jensen. Please have a seat.'

I sat in the traditional way, at floor level. She said something in Japanese to the happy housekeeper, who ran out of the room and appeared a few moments later with green tea and some strange-tasting little cakes. I tried the cakes but decided to just drink the tea.

'Yes, that's right,' I said. 'First of all, I'm sorry about your father's death, Miss Kawaguchi. I knew about him from his students and I once saw him give a demonstration. He was a great karateka. A great man.'

I thought this was a pretty good start. Diplomatic and polite, if I say so myself. To my surprise, Naoko just looked at me with no expression on her pale face.

'Yes ...' she said, 'but Miss Jensen, how can I help? I don't know anything about my father's murder.' Her voice was flat, without feeling.

'No, I know that, but I'm particularly interested in the connection with Murphy's hanging,' I said. I had tried the polite way and it hadn't worked. I decided to come straight to the point. I wouldn't be in Tokyo long and I had a lot to find out.

Naoko went even paler and looked away. 'It was all so long ago, Miss Jensen,' she said.

That phrase again! The pain from my head suddenly returned. I was beginning to lose my patience with this woman.

'Miss Kawaguchi,' I said firmly, 'it may have been a long time ago but your father has just been murdered and so has Hiromitsu Ito. Last night someone tried to threaten me with violence.' I was pointing to my bruise which by now was a dramatic purple with yellow edges. 'This is not a game. Something is going on and I intend to find out what.'

'What can I tell you?' she said. 'Murphy killed John – Mr Blakeston – and he shot me. I was sixteen years old. From that day I've been in a wheelchair. He killed a man and he was hanged. It was the law. What more can I say?' Her voice was cold, without feeling, but I noticed that her hands were shaking.

'When you gave the police a description of the killer, you said his hair was black. But then at the police station you picked out Murphy, whose hair was light brown. Couldn't you have made a mistake? Are you sure it was him, Miss Kawaguchi?'

I knew that this approach was risky, that she might just tell me to go away. I was right.

'Miss Jensen, it is over thirty years ago. Brendan Murphy is dead ... what's the point in bringing it all up again? Please leave me alone, Miss Jensen. I am not well ... I feel very tired.'

'Why did you come back to Japan, Miss Kawaguchi?' I asked. 'It can't be easy for you here. All your family are in England. Why didn't you stay near your brother?'

'Please go, Miss Jensen,' she said, starting to cry. She called for the housekeeper and I was asked to leave. The housekeeper was still smiling but it was clear that I had no choice but to go.

Chapter 9 *Naoko's story*

'Well,' I thought to myself, as I went home in the taxi, 'I certainly made a big mistake there!' Now what was I going to do? I had messed up with Naoko and I might not get another chance. I arrived back at the hotel feeling very tired and very angry with myself.

The Hotel Rhiga in the Waseda area of Tokyo was in what the Japanese think of as the European style. It was large and elegant with beautiful furniture and lots of gold paint. On the walls there were pictures of English gentlemen with hunting dogs and guns and, since it was Japan, there was recorded music everywhere, even in the lift. The music was designed not to annoy anyone which means that after a while you didn't notice it. Then your brain turned to water.

I went straight to my room to rest and think. The wallpaper was dark green and somehow comforting. I turned down the lights and listened to Pat Metheny on my walkman. I ordered some sushi[13] from room service then opened the mini bar and poured myself a beer. Sushi was my favourite food in the whole world but I ate without much appetite; I was so tired my body didn't know what time of day or night it was. I lay on the comfortable bed and closed my eyes. Suddenly the telephone was ringing on the bedside table. I felt like I had been drugged, then realised that I had been in a deep sleep. I jumped up and answered the phone.

45

'Moshi moshi,'[14] I said in my best Japanese, struggling into a dressing gown thoughtfully provided by the hotel.

It was Naoko Kawaguchi's happy housekeeper.

'Miss Jensen? Miss Kawaguchi would like to speak to you. She has something to tell you. She was a little upset before.'

'I'll be there in an hour,' I said, already grabbing a bath towel. I jumped into the shower and tried to wake myself up.

*   *   *

'Miss Jensen, I have never told anyone this, but I am dying. I'm afraid I may die and then no-one would ever know!' Naoko Kawaguchi was as pale as when I had left her. She had been crying a lot and her face was still wet with tears.

'What is it, Miss Kawaguchi? Is it something about Blakeston, about Blakeston's murder?' I asked.

'Miss Jensen, I have never told anyone this – John Blakeston was my lover!' she said quietly.

'Your lover?' I said. 'Well, people did wonder at the time, but you denied it, your parents denied it.'

'Of course, Miss Jensen,' she went on. 'My father is – was – a very dominating person. I loved my father, Miss Jensen, but I feared him. He was a strict man. A severe man, you might say. When he found out what was going on, he tried to stop me from seeing John. My father wanted to take me away from that school. He didn't want me to ruin my life.'

I remembered the photograph of Kawaguchi at Jun's

house. Yes, I could imagine that he was very strict with his children. Particularly with his daughter perhaps.

'You were very young . . .' I started carefully.

'I was nearly seventeen and Blakeston was twenty . . . just twenty years old.' Naoko started crying again.

'The worst thing . . . the thing that gives me nightmares,' cried the poor woman, 'is that I'm not sure that it was Brendan Murphy who killed John. I wasn't sure then and I'm still not sure. I'm terribly afraid, Miss Jensen, that I sent an innocent man to his death!'

'But Miss Kawaguchi, you picked him out at the police station, you gave evidence against him in court.'

'Miss Jensen,' she replied. 'I was young, very young. I loved John very much. He was the only man who had ever shown me any kindness. I was terribly upset, in shock. It was a terrible experience. Can you imagine what it was like for a sixteen-year-old girl? It was hard for me to remember what really happened. I had spent five hours in a car with a madman and seen John murdered. I had been shot three times in the back and was lucky to be alive.'

I thought for a while. Murphy's guilt was almost totally based on what Naoko Kawaguchi had said. If she had made a mistake . . .

'But you must have got a really good look at the man during the five hours you were in the car with him,' I said.

'Not really, Miss Jensen,' she explained. 'He was in the back seat the whole time and remember it was dark for a lot of the time. Oh, I have no doubt that the murderer looked something like Murphy, but I'm no surer than that.'

A lot of people looked like Murphy, I thought.

'Then my father was so insistent,' she continued. 'He

wanted the whole thing to be finished. He didn't want anyone to know that John and I were . . .'

'Miss Kawaguchi,' I said, 'think carefully before you answer this . . . is it possible that your father had John Blakeston killed?'

'I am afraid that I have thought about this many times, Miss Jensen,' she replied. 'I don't know. I don't know . . . I just don't know.' And with that, she started crying again.

On the way back to the hotel in the taxi, I thought about Naoko's story. I thought I now understood why Naoko preferred to live in Japan. At least she was far away from the memories of her terrible experience so many years ago. Far away, until curious reporters like me came to find her, to make her talk about it all again. Sometimes I hated my job.

I thought too about her father. Kawaguchi had not wanted his daughter to ruin her life by getting involved with an older man. Perhaps he had also felt that Blakeston was not good enough for his beloved daughter. A caretaker would hardly be the right person for a Kawaguchi. And she was very young. Perhaps he feared that the girl would get pregnant and have to have the baby. It would have ruined her life perhaps. But if he had had Blakeston killed he had ruined his daughter's life anyway. The murderer had either gone mad and shot Naoko too or had just made a mistake. Either way, Naoko had ended up losing the person she loved and being in a wheelchair for the rest of her life. It was a tragedy whichever way you looked at it.

27th December 1960
Brixton Prison

Dear Mum and Dad

It was wonderful to see you yesterday and to know that you are well. That is the main thing for me at this time, believe me.

Mr Jeffreys came today and told me that we should hear the result of the appeal to the Home Secretary any day now. He is a fine man and I know he is doing his very best for me. We are trying to prove that I was in Manchester when this terrible crime happened. Unfortunately, it is not so easy to prove as the people who I met there have disappeared and cannot be traced.

There must be somebody out there who knows that I am in this dreadful situation and could come forward and save me. That's the thing I can't understand — why they are keeping quiet. Some days I go mad just thinking about it.

I hope that Johnny has been to see you and he is providing you with some comfort through this terrible ordeal. Please believe that it will soon be over and that I'll be home, where I belong. The thought of that is the only thing that keeps me going.

From your loving son

Brendan

That night I felt low – a combination of the time difference and the interview with Naoko Kawaguchi, whose life seemed like a living hell. My mind went over and over what she had told me. It was much too busy to feel sleepy. I went for a swim in the hotel pool to try and tire myself out. Fifty lengths later I still felt low but at least I was exhausted; I might have some chance of sleeping. I lay on my bed and thought a lot about fathers and daughters. Naoko's relationship to her father was so different to the one between Dad and me. Perhaps Kawaguchi had loved her so much that he wouldn't let her make any mistakes at all. It was like he wanted to protect her from life itself. Unfortunately, his dominating attitude had meant that she had possibly made an even worse mistake. She had given evidence that Murphy was the murderer and sent him to his death.

How different to Dad, I thought. He would never actually stop me from doing anything that I really wanted to do. He would advise me, guide me, but never dominate me. I thought about the times in the past when he had let me do things which were risky or even dangerous. When I was a teenager I had done all kinds of risky things, like most teenagers I suppose. The usual kind of stuff – drugs, drink – the things that most of my generation fell into.

Now I realised that he must have suffered watching me, knowing that it could all turn out badly, that he might lose me. But he knew that I had to work it out for myself, that if he tried to stop me I would just want to do it more. I smiled to myself. I hadn't turned out too badly. Now I never took drugs, not even an aspirin, and only drank socially.

They were two very different ways of loving someone I suppose, Kawaguchi's and Dad's. I went to sleep feeling very lucky.

Chapter 10   *A visit to a Japanese dojo*

I didn't have much time left in Tokyo and I knew that I had got everything I could hope for from Naoko Kawaguchi. I decided to do some sightseeing and went to the Asakusa area of the city to visit the Asakusa Kannon Temple and to walk round its lively streets.

I had come to a dojo in this old area of the city with my club once before. I loved this part of Tokyo, with its hundreds of tiny old shops and its crowds of people. I walked down the main street, Nakamise-dori, and spent an hour or so looking into the shops with their mixture of traditional Japanese clothes and cheap souvenirs. I bought things to take home. As I walked round the side streets, there were smells of interesting food coming from the restaurants and I realised that I was beginning to get very hungry.

I walked through a cloth-covered doorway into a little traditional noodle house. The waiter came almost immediately with some green tea and I ordered my favourite sansai soba, delicious noodles with mountain vegetables. I picked up my wooden chopsticks and was just about to start eating when I heard someone call 'Kate-san, Kate-san!'

I looked up towards the doorway and saw the smiling face of a young Japanese man in his late twenties. I looked at him carefully for some time before finally recognising him. It was Kenji, one of the students of the dojo where we had trained. I smiled and stood up, offering my hand and then quickly remembering that I was in Japan and should bow.

Kenji laughed. 'Kate-san!' he said, 'What a surprise! What are you doing here? Are you training?' He sat down and ordered some noodles and I told him about the story I was doing for the newspaper and about my visit to Naoko Kawaguchi. Kenji ate his noodles noisily and his eyes got bigger and bigger as he listened to my story.

Finally he finished his noodles and said: 'That's quite a story, Kate. But you should be careful. You might get hurt – it sounds like someone is desperate. Now, what are you doing this afternoon? Why don't you come and visit the dojo? There's a training session and I'm sure Ando-sensei will be delighted to see you again. You must come.'

Kenji was so enthusiastic about his idea and I couldn't think of a good reason why I shouldn't go to the dojo. My flight was a late one and I had plenty of time. It would be good to see everyone again and to forget about Naoko Kawaguchi for a while. We left the restaurant and Kenji led me through the narrow streets to the traditional Yotsuya dojo in the oldest part of Asakusa.

I looked around at the familiar dojo with its wooden floor and its Japanese characters on the wall. On entering the dojo you had to take off your shoes before stepping onto the polished wood of the floor. I recognised many of the students and they came to bow to me, shyly. I approached Ando-sensei and greeted him. He recognised me and smiled in a friendly way. In many traditional dojos, the sensei doesn't allow people to come and just watch training sessions. Anybody who is inside the dojo must be training. But in this case Ando-sensei gave me special permission to watch and I was grateful.

The training, as always in this dojo, was hard and intense. Training of the spirit and of the mind was as important as training of the body. The students performed the traditional two kneeling bows, one to the dojo, the other to the sensei. Then the lines of students went up and down the dojo to the sensei's commands, doing their basic punches and kicks, their eyes fixed ahead of them. Any student who lost his concentration was punished with extra physical exercises. Ando-sensei was a tough teacher, though he was always fair.

The best part of the session for me was the kata. The kata is a series of fighting moves that each student performs on his own against an imaginary opponent. It is beautiful to watch when performed well, rather like a classical dance. And here it was performed well, by Ando-sensei's most advanced students, Kenji among them. Once they had finished the long kata, called 'Kushanku', there was stillness and calm. But although their bodies had stopped moving, the energy still flowed. In Japanese, this energy was called 'zanshin'. It was a word made up of two Japanese characters 'zan', which means to continue and 'shin' which means heart or spirit. I thought of Kawaguchi-sensei again and his club, Zanshin. I wondered whether his spirit would continue in the club, even though he was dead.

After the session, I went for tea with Ando-sensei and Kenji to a nearby teashop. Ando-sensei was keen to hear my story. He listened very carefully, then after some time he said. 'You know, Kate-san, the true budoka[15] or student of the martial arts, does not need to attack. The art is in waiting for your opponent to attack and then using his own energy to beat him. It seems to me that your murderer is moving towards you. Remember always to get off the line of attack, but keep close to him so that you can catch him when the time is right.'

Chapter 11   *A drink at The Penguin*

Back in London the police were still busy interviewing karate people in London who had a police record for violence. After my interview with Naoko Kawaguchi, I was convinced that there was some connection to the London Road murder. It was so long ago, but somebody was making sure that we remembered it.

I knew that I now had to set about finding Benson – the man who had confessed to killing Blakeston – if he was still alive. I could always go to police records, but the problem was that that would attract people's attention, which I didn't want. After the attack I had decided to be more careful.

'Why don't you start at The Penguin in Fleet Street?' Dad suggested. 'It's still there; I saw something about it in the newspaper the other day. Benson used to drink there. But remember, we're talking about a long time ago. Years ago.'

It seemed as good a place as any. I took another look at the photograph of Benson in the "Who Killed Murphy?" book and headed off to Fleet Street.

In the days when the British newspaper industry was centred on Fleet Street, The Penguin was the bar where all the journalists used to go to drink and chat. Dad talked of a time when the place was buzzing with hundreds of reporters, always onto something new, always chasing a story. These days I guessed it was a pretty sad place compared to then. It was mostly used by young executives with mobile phones and secretaries from the offices in the area.

When I got there it was early evening and The Penguin was full of people who had stopped in for a drink after work. The place was noisy and crowded and full of smoke. I was hoping I wouldn't have to stay long. I didn't feel very hopeful about finding Benson – it was all so long ago. I was even starting to use that phrase myself.

I got myself a beer and stood at the bar. All the seats were taken so it was the only place to be. I like standing at the bar anyway; all the most interesting conversation happens there. I looked around. It was a typical central London pub; dark wood and big mirrors everywhere. There were dark red leather seats under the mirrors and small round tables here and there.

I looked back to the people behind the bar. There were three of them: a middle-aged woman and two young men. The woman had a friendly face, bright red lipstick and a lot of messy blonde hair. She moved quickly behind the bar, a true professional. She looked like the best person to talk to.

I watched out for a break in the constant serving of drinks and jumped in quickly and started to make conversation.

'This place must have changed a lot since the old days,' I said, smiling at her. 'My Dad used to come here thirty years ago, when it was all reporters.'

Thankfully, she smiled back and started chatting. She was a friendly kind of woman.

'It's changed even in my day, love!' she said. 'My God, how it's changed . . . and not for the better, I tell you.' At this point she lowered her voice as if she were going to tell me a big secret. 'Between you and me,' she said, 'I'd much rather have journalists than this lot.' She nodded her head in the direction of the bar. A smart young man in an executive suit was holding a five pound note up and saying something.

'What's that love?' she called to him, 'a pint of bitter, right you are my darling,' and she moved quickly to the other end of the bar to serve the young man. Once she had pulled the pint of beer and taken his money she came back.

'Yes,' I said, as casually as possible, 'he used to know somebody called Peter . . . Benson, I think his name was. Used to drink here. But he lost touch with him.'

'Yes . . . well, a lot of the old crowd left, you know,' she replied. 'When they moved the newspaper offices. A journalist was he, this friend of your Dad's?'

'No, I don't think so,' I said. 'But I think a lot of his friends were journalists. An odd chap apparently. A bit strange, you know. But he must be about seventy now, perhaps older.'

'Oh . . . I think I know who you mean, love. A bit crazy. Yeah, yeah. I think he sometimes drinks at that pub just round the corner. The Six Bells. Left here years ago, he did. Had a bit of an argument with the old landlord. Something about a bet on a horse. Complete madman.' She tapped her head. It could mean anything, that sign, from slightly strange to completely mad. And with that she moved off to the other end of the bar to serve another group of customers.

I finished my beer and went out into the cold evening

air of central London in search of The Six Bells. It was easy to find. It was, as the woman had said, just round the corner. I looked up at the old pub sign hanging outside, six gold bells on a dark blue background. The pub itself looked very old, as if it desperately needed repairs.

I bought myself another beer and found a seat. Although only three minutes walk from The Penguin, The Six Bells was very different. By now it was 7.30 and there were four customers in the public bar. They looked like regulars. They weren't talking to each other. Three of them stood at the bar with their pints of beer. The fourth, an elderly man, was sitting at a small table. The barman looked like he hadn't shaved for days and had just got out of bed. I told him that I was looking for Peter Benson.

'Oh, he stopped coming here about last November,' the barman said. 'I don't know whether he died or what. He was completely mad, you know.'

My heart sank. Benson might be dead! What I had feared all along might be true. If so, it was going to be more difficult than I thought.

'He's got a brother living in London somewhere, though,' the barman added. 'Here, that chap over there might know where he lives – he knew him.'

The barman pointed in the direction of one of the four regulars, the elderly man sitting in the other corner of the bar drinking Guinness. The old man did know James Benson, Peter's brother, and said he lived in Islington, in North London. He didn't know the exact address, but he thought it was off Upper Street. He used to drink with Benson at The Six Bells sometimes. It was a chance; the brother might know nothing at all, but I knew I had to try.

5th January 1961
Brixton Prison

Dear Paddy

Paddy, you have got to be strong at this time, especially for Mum and Dad and Ian. By now you will know that my appeal has failed and they have set the hanging date for 4th February. Mr Jeffreys came to tell me yesterday. Since then my mind has been spinning as you can imagine. I have hardly slept, going through this thing over and over in my head. I can't really tell you how a man feels at a time like this, only that it's the most terrible feeling in the world.

Mr Jeffreys will try everything he knows. The only hope is an appeal for a reprieve to the Home Secretary. But I don't know how much real hope there is now, unless the real murderer comes forward and gives himself up. Somebody, somewhere, did this crime and I am paying for it.

Be brave Paddy and pray for me.

Your loving brother

Brendan

Chapter 12 *A very strange man*

I found James Benson in a rather nice flat just off Upper Street, as the old guy in the pub had said. He wasn't at all what I expected. He was a man of about seventy, very smartly dressed in dark suit and tie. The large modern flat was furnished well and there were expensive paintings around the walls – signs of a man of learning and culture. He spoke rather like a retired lawyer or country doctor.

'Come in, Miss Jensen, come in. That old Peter story coming up again eh?'

He smiled kindly. I had told him the minimum of details on the phone.

'Peter died last year,' he told me. 'He was a very strange man. He was my brother, you understand, but I have to say he was odd. Some very strange ideas. But could be very amusing, you know.' Benson smiled, as if remembering one of his brother's jokes.

A laugh a minute, I thought, but said: 'A lot of people seem to think he killed John Blakeston, Mr Benson.'

'Well, you know I suppose that he confessed once himself, after Murphy had been hanged?' Benson said.

'Yes, I do know that,' I went on. 'What do you think, Mr Benson? Did he do it? Is there a chance that he did it?'

'Well you know, Miss Jensen, the honest truth is that there certainly is a chance. He said a lot of different things at different times. At one time he claimed that the father –

Kawaguchi the name was, wasn't it? – had asked him to frighten Blakeston off. Kawaguchi got to know Peter through a friend of a friend. I can't remember who now. Kawaguchi was really worried about his daughter who was seeing this young Blakeston. The girl was young, I think he was afraid she would get pregnant, ruin her life.'

'It sounds a bit unlikely. Why didn't Kawaguchi scare him off himself? After all, he was a karate expert,' I interrupted.

'Ah, my dear young lady, subtlety was needed,' Benson explained. 'I think the story was that the father had tried everything – talked to his daughter, to the young man, but he hadn't succeeded. He was desperate. This was a last attempt.'

If Kawaguchi had wanted Benson because he thought he would be subtle, I thought, he had certainly made a mistake.

'But why your brother?' I asked.

'Well, again I don't know exactly,' Benson smiled. 'But Peter went through a very moral period. He saw himself as a kind of moral avenger, someone who rights wrongs.'

That word "avenger" again.

'And he was very friendly, you know,' Benson smiled again. 'He always seemed so normal, so reasonable.'

'But he wasn't?'

'Nobody could claim that my brother was normal or reasonable. I think he was what modern psychiatrists call a psychopath; in other words a madman.' Benson stopped.

'Psychopath is a bit of an overused word,' I said.

'Well, Peter was a professional liar, and had little or no concern for the suffering of others. On top of that he followed only his own desires. I think you will find that these qualities, if you can call them that, are the signs of a psychopath. I speak as a retired psychologist.'

So as a professional James Benson would know what he was talking about. And like a professional he sounded cold, almost without feeling. I wondered how he had really felt about his brother. Peter sounded like a monster.

'Mr Benson, do you think there's a chance that Kawaguchi paid your brother to kill Blakeston?' I asked.

'What, and hurt his daughter?' Benson replied in surprise. 'No, no, Miss Jensen, I don't think so. I think that Peter intended to frighten Blakeston. Kawaguchi may have said something directly to him, or Peter may have thought that he should do that. He took the gun. Remember that they drove around for hours, with Peter talking to them. Peter could talk, my God he could talk! Then what may have happened is that Blakeston got frightened and made a sudden movement. Peter panicked and shot him. Then the whole thing just got worse. Peter didn't know anything about guns, I'm sure of that. It was the first time in his life he'd ever used one as far as I know.'

'Then the whole thing was a tragic mistake?' I asked.

'That is my reading of the situation, Miss Jensen.'

'Mr Benson, you're talking as if there's no doubt in your mind that your brother committed this crime,' I said slowly.

'That's right, Miss Jensen, there is very little doubt,' Benson replied. 'I think it's highly probable that Peter killed Blakeston, and shot Miss Kawaguchi. He may not have intended to at first, but that's what probably happened.'

'But Mr Benson, if you knew that your brother had committed the crime, why didn't you come forward and tell the police? Why did you hide your brother?' I asked.

James Benson looked at me seriously. 'I didn't hide him, Miss Jensen. I told the police on more than one occasion. I couldn't be one hundred per cent sure, but I thought it highly probable that my brother did it. Either they didn't believe me or they just didn't want to know.'

This was getting more and more interesting. I could understand why people would not believe Peter Benson. He had obviously been crazy. But James Benson? This man was highly intelligent and completely normal. Why had the police not taken any notice of him?

I wondered how Murphy had come into the story. Was he someone who just happened to be in the wrong place at the wrong time? Did the police just pick him up? Kawaguchi and Benson would have been happy that they suspected someone else. Or did Benson know him? Did Benson in fact set Murphy up and make the police believe that Murphy was the murderer?

'And what about Murphy?' I asked.

'Ah, there, Miss Jensen, I really don't know the answer. I don't know if my brother knew him. I'm sure the authorities know all about this, Miss Jensen. But they hanged Murphy for the murder – you can hardly expect them to admit that they made a mistake.'

15th January 1961
Brixton Prison

Dear Janey

Thanks for your letter which I received yesterday. Things are pretty tough, here, as you can imagine, though the prison officers treat me well. I like to think it's because they know I'm innocent.

My solicitor, Mr Jeffreys, is working night and day to find a way out of this dreadful mess. I don't know what to do except keep saying that I'm innocent. I just keep thinking about what I'll do when I get out, just to get me through it. I try to keep cheerful, but it isn't easy, with nobody believing you.

The only thing that keeps me going is the thought that I might have some kind of life with you when I'm finally out of here.

I'm looking forward to seeing you on Friday.

Yours

Brendan

Chapter 13   *The Avenger strikes*

That night I had some thinking to do. If, as James Benson guessed, his brother had panicked and killed Blakeston, Kawaguchi had certainly made a serious mistake. He had put his trust in a man who could not be trusted and he, Kawaguchi, was therefore indirectly responsible for the terrible crime that had followed. But who was The Avenger? And was he or she avenging Blakeston's death, the shooting of Naoko or the hanging of Murphy? So many questions and so few answers.

The next day, though, something happened which gave the whole thing a different direction and which answered at least some of these questions.

It was about 9.30 in the morning. I was sitting at my desk in the office, talking to Rick about a story he was working on. Suddenly the phone rang and there was Jonty from police headquarters, breathless with excitement.

'The Home Secretary ...' he said. 'There's been a letter bomb ... luckily it was discovered by his assistant before being opened. There'll be an official statement soon I suppose.'

A few minutes later a statement from the Home Secretary's office came through on the fax.

'A letter bomb was discovered in the Home Secretary's post this morning. The Home Secretary's assistant,

Jonathon Bailey, discovered the suspicious-looking package. No-one was hurt in the incident.'

About ten minutes later there was another fax, this time from Reuters News Agency.

'At 9.30 this morning we received a handwritten note from someone calling himself The Avenger. He said he was responsible for the letter bomb delivered this morning to the Home Secretary's home. He said that Murphy was innocent and he would avenge his death.'

I got onto Reuters News Agency and asked them whether they were sure it was a man. No, they weren't – they'd just assumed it was. I asked to see the note, to get our people to look at the handwriting.

I rushed down to the Home Secretary's office in Downing Street to see if I could get a story from Jonathon Bailey. I had a contact at Downing Street, so managed to get a short interview with him.

'Nothing much to say, really,' he said. 'This brown paper package arrived. Something about it made me suspicious, so I called the police. Then they called in the bomb squad.' He made it sound like it happened every day. Possibly it did.

I spent the rest of the morning at the Public Records Office reading the reports of the two public enquiries into the Murphy case. Both found 'no evidence to support the re-opening of the case'. Yes, well, there wasn't much point, given that Murphy was dead. John Murphy, Brendan's father had asked for a pardon on five separate occasions between 1963 and 1970. He had been denied on each occasion. In 1965 a committee made up of five public figures had put forward a document to the Home Secretary, stating that there was a sufficient reason to re-open the case as Peter Benson had confessed. It too had been denied. Even after Peter Benson's confession!

As late as 1992, there had been a call for a public enquiry made to the Home Secretary. He had made a statement in the House of Commons, saying that there was absolutely no reason for another public enquiry. In his opinion there was no new evidence in the case. Since then there had been nothing. Most of the people involved in trying to clear Murphy's name were now dead. Dad was the only one still alive.

3rd February 1961
Brixton Prison

Dear Mum and Dad

Well, it has finally come to this. It is hard for me to put together this letter as I am sure you know. I have been sitting here for hours and wondering how it came to this – how I got into this situation – but no answer comes to me.

The priest, Father Daly, has come to see me every day this week. He is a kind man and has talked to me a lot. I know that he knows that I am innocent and this knowledge helps me more than anything at this time. He will be with me to the end and is helping me to be brave.

I want you to remember always that I didn't do this and that I am being punished for something I never did, that I am innocent. I hope that when I am dead you will continue to fight to clear my name and to prove that I never did it. More than anything I don't want you to blame yourselves for what has happened because you have really been the best parents in the world.

Tomorrow I hope that when the time comes I will go to my death bravely. I want you to be proud of me to the end. Thinking of you and Paddy and Ian helps me a lot at this time. God bless you all.

Your loving son

Brendan

Chapter 14 *A hell of a fighter*

At lunch time I met Jonty in our usual bar in Piccadilly. He seemed even more nervous than usual. I assumed that the reason for this was that the police weren't getting any further with the Kawaguchi and Ito murder cases. He was wearing a pink tie with the Pink Panther on it. I tried not to look too disgusted, but my face must have shown something because he looked at the tie and smiled stupidly.

'Ah . . . birthday present,' he said. I didn't trust myself to speak.

Finally I said, 'Jonty, I spoke to James Benson, Peter's brother. He's almost certain that his brother committed the murder. He told me that he had told the police a few times. Do you know anything about it?'

'Not much,' Jonty said. 'I just think that the evidence against Murphy was so strong . . . '

I remembered Dad telling me about the Manchester alibi. There was hardly any evidence against Murphy.

'So what do you know about public enquiries into the London Road murder case?' I asked. 'Surely the police must be aware of the connection with Kawaguchi?'

'I don't think anybody is very keen to look into the Murphy case again. There have already been two public enquiries,' he said, smoking his usual Rothmans, 'which both concluded that Murphy was the London Road murderer. But they're going to have to do something. This

Avenger is really hotting up. Two murders and the attempted murder of the Home Secretary. Not bad for ten days' work.'

I rarely expected Jonty to tell me anything I didn't already know. He, on his side, rarely disappointed me.

I finished my beer and stood up to go. If Jonty knew anything, he would say it now. Jonty said nothing, apart from 'bye-bye', and I left for the office. I was no nearer to knowing who The Avenger was, even though he or she (I was beginning to feel with more certainty that this person was a woman) definitely knew who I was. It was an uncomfortable feeling.

Back at the office I got down to some serious thinking. I had given the handwriting sample from the letter bomb to our handwriting expert, Sandra Watts. She was a careful woman who never spoke before being absolutely certain. 'Well, Kate,' she said, 'in my opinion there's a seventy-five per cent chance that it's a woman.'

'Can you tell her age?' I asked. 'Not exactly, but certainly not older than forty. You generally don't find this style of handwriting in people over forty.'

I was now almost sure that she was a woman. Fairly young – no older than her early thirties, judging by her attack on me. If it was her who attacked me. She wasn't alive at the time of the London Road murder, or only just. My age, in other words. Perhaps she was a relative of Brendan Murphy's. But who? I rang the information department upstairs to ask them to find out about any female relatives of Brendan Murphy, however distant, of that age. They came up with zero. But then suddenly I had an idea . . .

I rang Paddy Murphy in Peterborough.

'Mr Murphy, you said Brendan had lots of girlfriends,' I began. 'Can you remember any of their names?'

Paddy Murphy laughed.

'Good Lord, Miss Jensen. Brendan had so many girlfriends. It'd take me a week to tell you all their names, even if could remember them. He was what you might call a ladies' man.'

'But was there any one in particular, Mr Murphy, just one who might have been special, who perhaps lasted longer than the others?'

Paddy Murphy thought for a while.

'Well, the only one I can remember at all is Janey Lovat. She used to live near us. I can remember her because Brendan always used to call her "Lovely Lovat". He was a bit of a joker.'

Lovat. Not a terribly common name. I looked at the list of registered black belts in London. There were two Lovats. One Brian Lovat, 2nd dan, who trained in Wimbledon, the other Brenda Lovat, 4th dan, who was a member of the Zanshin Karate club, Kawaguchi-sensei's club. The name was familiar. I rang Sanjay and confirmed it was who I thought it was. Brenda Lovat was a top fighter – one of the top three women fighters in the country. I had seen her in the Internationals once; she was in Ticky Donovan's team fighting for Great Britain. She was a hell of a fighter.

I thought back to Ando-sensei's advice to me when I was in Tokyo. 'Keep off the line of attack and wait until the time is right,' he had said. I had a strong feeling that the time had now come. If my guess was right, The Avenger was fighting a single-handed battle against everyone – the police, the government, the whole world. It was a lonely business: perhaps she would be glad of some company. I had an idea, but first I had to get Balzano to agree to it – and Dad.

Chapter 15   *Right hook*

The next morning Dad's name appeared in The Daily Echo for the first time in twenty years. It was a risk but if it worked it would be worth it. The article was Dad at his best. It began:

Judicial Murder?
by Tony Jensen

Was Brendan Murphy the London Road murderer or not? More than thirty years ago, when I was the first reporter on the scene of this dreadful crime, I said that he was not the murderer. Today, however, I feel differently . . .

He went on to describe his part in the reporting of the crime, the trial and the hanging. He explained the doubts he and others had then about the result of the trial. Then he went on to explain why there had been an attempt to kill the Home Secretary just two days before. And finally about how he had changed his mind about Brendan Murphy's guilt, how he now thought that Murphy was responsible for the London Road murder. Classic Tony Jensen, except that the last part was a pack of lies.

I hardly dared to believe that it would work.

I phoned Sanjay and explained my plan, asking him if he would help. He accepted gladly, as I knew he would. 'What fun!' he said and I could imagine his eyes shining as he said it. 'Fun' was not exactly the word I would have used, but I was glad that Sanjay would be there.

That evening we were both at Dad's house. Sanjay was in the kitchen with the lights off and I was at the top of the stairs, hidden behind an old wardrobe. Dad sat in the living room in his usual chair, reading. It was six o'clock and already black outside. It was a typical winter evening in London – freezing cold and wet. We had no idea how long we would have to wait. Perhaps all evening. Perhaps all night. But something told me that the time was right and that our avenger would attack.

The main thing was to protect Dad, to make sure that he came to no harm. It was a big risk – too big really – but I knew it was one I had to take. Dad was as relaxed as ever about it; as usual he had no fear of danger. I was the nervous one.

The silence seemed to go on for hours. It was so quiet that I could hear the ticking of the big clock in the sitting room and Dad occasionally turning the pages of his book. Sanjay was quiet behind the kitchen door and I tried to move as little as possible. I had given Dad strict instructions not to move at all, whatever happened. Finally, just before seven, the silence was broken.

The first I knew about it was a signal from Sanjay, a sharp 'kiai'.[16] Sanjay's shout was the most terrifying thing you could imagine and it sent me rushing down the stairs as fast as I could move to find Sanjay struggling with someone. By that time Sanjay had attacked the person from behind and there was quite a fight going on. The lights in the hall were not bright and it was difficult to see. The person was slim and small, dressed all in black. On his or her head – it was impossible to tell whether it was a man or a woman – was a black cap which covered all the face apart from the eyes. It was the type used by climbers – or burglars. The only thing you could see was the eyes. I went to help.

By this time, we were in the hall just outside the living room where Dad was sitting. I went for the person's legs and managed to hold on for a few seconds while Sanjay put his arm around the person's throat from behind. The best way to release yourself from this hold is with a sharp elbow strike back into the opponent's body, which happened so fast that Sanjay had no time to react. He was hit, but the hit wasn't direct and Sanjay managed to hold on again. Suddenly there was a movement from the living room. 'Oh no,' I thought, 'It's Dad!'

Dad came out of the living room just as Sanjay had managed to put his arm back around the person's neck. Time seemed to slow down as I wondered whether to stop Dad and risk letting go of the person. I paused, unsure of what to do. Meanwhile, Dad pulled his arm back, aimed at the person's face and delivered one of his famous right hooks. It was not quite as powerful as it had been, but it was powerful enough. The person went down and fell to the floor, out cold.

'I thought I told you not to move,' I smiled at Dad, 'but that was a bloody good right hook.'

I lifted the cap and looked at the woman's face underneath, now asleep as if she had just decided to take a rest. The pale skin and brown eyes looked very like the photograph of Brendan Murphy I had seen recently.

'Let's carry her through to the living room and tie her

up in case she wakes up,' I said, not wishing to go through all that again. Dad brought a rope and Sanjay tied her up to a chair at the wrists and feet. I didn't want to phone the police yet – there were a few things I needed to know first.

'Brenda Lovat, I assume,' I said, as soon as she opened her eyes. She nodded once and looked at me straight in the eyes.

'Yeah,' she said, in her strong south London accent. 'What about it?'

3rd February 1961
Brixton Prison

Dear Janey

This is going to be a very difficult letter because I won't be able to say all the things I really want to say. You will just have to read between the lines.

Well, all my appeals have failed and the end is now very close. I have lived in hope for so long, but now I have no hope left. I don't think anything or anyone can save me. The lawyers have done their best but it's all over.

Janey, you must think about the future and try to forget about all this. It won't be easy at first, but you must try. I know that life is going to be hard for you and I can't tell you how terrible I feel about it all. Please carry on believing that I didn't commit this terrible crime. Remember also that I never wanted to give you all this trouble. I hope that you will be strong at this time for me and for yourself.

I'll be thinking of you tomorrow. God bless you.

Love

Brendan

Chapter 16 *Fathers and daughters*

Dad made some tea and we sat in his living room drinking it. It could have been a social visit, the height of normality, except that Lovat was tied to a chair with rope. She was unable to move, apart from her right hand and arm, which she was using to lift her teacup.

'Mum had only just found out she was going to have a baby when Brendan was picked up by the police,' she said. 'Nobody knew about it, only Brendan, and they decided not to tell anyone, not even his family. There's no mention of it in his letters from prison because the prison officers would have read the letters. Before you knew it everyone in the country would have known.'

I nodded and waited.

Brenda continued, 'They wanted to wait until he was free before they told everyone. They thought it would only be a few weeks, perhaps a month or so. How could they imagine that it would go on so long and end like that? It was incredible. Mum moved away a month or so later and I was born when my father had already been hanged.'

'And she brought you up, without anyone guessing the truth?' I asked.

'Yeah, it was easy,' Brenda replied. 'His family hardly knew Mum anyway and no-one guessed. Of course we used Mum's name – they weren't married anyway. At first, when I was a kid, she told me that Dad had died just before I was born. But later she told me the truth. I was probably about twelve when she told me.' Brenda looked sad. 'I still remember the day,' she said.

'And you wanted to avenge his death.' It was half question, half statement. Brenda looked at me.

'You don't know what it's like growing up like that. My father had been hanged for something he never did. You have to understand. Look at the case – the prosecution had no evidence. There is no evidence, that's the truth of it,' she said, looking over at Dad. Dad looked at her kindly. He knew she was right.

'He was a victim,' Brenda continued. 'The authorities made a mistake and because he came from a poor family with no power, he wasn't important. They just thought that if they kept quiet about it, everyone would forget. Well, they didn't know about me!' Brenda Lovat spoke passionately and I couldn't help admiring her.

'As I grew up I got more and more angry about it, about not having a dad.' She looked at Dad again as she said this. I could tell he was moved and did not trust himself to speak. 'I grew up poor and angry. Not easy. Mum tried her best, but it was hard, bloody hard.'

'I started training with Kawaguchi when I was about fourteen. By then I knew who he was, that was why I went there. I knew that he had thought that my father was guilty and was partly responsible for the whole thing. I knew him but he didn't know me,' she continued. 'He trained me well, I was good at it and I became a fighter.'

'So well that you could eventually kill him,' I said quietly.

Kawaguchi had been Lovat's sensei. Sensei in Japanese means much more than teacher, though it is often translated in that way. The sensei is the one who leads you along the way – the 'do'. In the world of martial arts, it was incredible that anyone could kill their sensei, unthinkable. Yet she had done it.

'I didn't hate Kawaguchi,' she said, as if reading my mind. 'I admired him for what he was – a truly great karateka – and thought he had made a mistake in trying to protect his daughter. It was all a dreadful, terrible mistake. I don't think he was an evil man – he just made an error of judgement. And he wasn't brave enough to admit it. That was his greatest mistake. A bit like the government, when you come to think of it – not big enough to admit that they made a mistake in killing Dad.'

I could see the similarity.

Lovat drank some tea and then continued: 'I didn't mean to kill him at first, I swear. I tried to tell the police what really happened, that Benson had killed Blakeston and that Dad was innocent. I wrote letters to Kawaguchi to get him to tell the police. I couldn't talk to him because I didn't want him to know who I was. I begged him but he didn't want to know. In the end I had to kill him.'

'You killed your own sensei!' Sanjay came in, clearly finding it incredible. Lovat nodded.

'And Ito?' I asked.

'Ito knew all about the letters. He had told the police and I was sure they'd find me,' she replied.

It was strange and disturbing how normal all this sounded. It was likely that the whole sad story had disturbed Brenda Lovat's mind and she had gone mad with the need for revenge.

'You're never going to bring your father back,' Dad said, not unkindly.

'No,' said Lovat, 'but I can make them listen. I want to get an official pardon. He deserves it. Can't you see that? He deserves it!'

I looked at Dad and thought what it would have been like not to know him. It was hard to imagine. I found it hard to judge Brenda Lovat badly for what she had done; if I'd been in the same situation, would I have done the same thing myself? It was hard to know, hard to understand exactly what she had lived through. It was hard to say how any individual might react to those circumstances. I could also see how the idea of an official pardon made her do it. Her father was gone forever – she would never get him back. But to clear his name – that was a fine goal, the only possible goal now, thirty-five years after Brendan's death.

'I tried for years to achieve a pardon for Brendan Murphy too,' said Dad, sadly. 'I devoted some years to it. It's not easy. It's so long ago – there can be no forensic evidence now.'

I had read something about this in "Who Killed Murphy?". The murderer had spent about five hours in the car with John Blakeston and Naoko Kawaguchi. This meant that there should have been something to prove that he had been there – sweat, hair, threads from his clothes, anything. Forensic evidence. Yet at Brendan Murphy's trial the prosecution did not produce any forensic evidence against him. There was nothing to positively prove that Murphy had been in the car. In fact, the only real evidence they had was Naoko Kawaguchi's word, the word of a terrified girl who had since doubted that it was Brendan at all.

But Dad was right of course – it was too late for all that now. No judge would accept evidence thirty-five years after the crime, even if Naoko Kawaguchi had changed her mind. The only way now to prove Murphy's innocence was to somehow prove the Manchester alibi, to prove that Murphy had been two hundred miles away when the crime was committed. It would not be easy; many people had tried to do this before and had failed.

'And now you've changed your mind!' said Lovat, looking at my Dad with contempt.

'No, no. I haven't changed my mind,' said Dad, sadly, 'It was just the only way we could bring you to us, to stop the murders ... and your pain. I still believe your father was innocent, Brenda. No, more than that. I KNOW your father was innocent.'

'Then DO something. Get a pardon for him. You have the facts, you're a journalist, do something!' Lovat almost screamed.

By now Sanjay had phoned the police and a few moments later we heard two cars screeching to a halt outside, blue lights flashing. I knew we had to hand her over, had to stop it once and for all, for her sake as much as anything. But we also owed her something. Before handing her over, Dad and I promised that we would do everything in our power to prove her father's innocence and gain an official pardon.

Brenda Lovat sat in the back of one of the police cars, looking as proud as ever. Jonty was in Dad's living room.

His orange and blue striped tie seemed disgusting in the circumstances.

'She's going to prison for a hell of a long time,' he said with pleasure in his voice, 'Two murders and the attempted murder of the Home Secretary. Wow!!'

'Yes, well,' I said, in a tired voice, 'I personally hope she won't be in prison for long. After all, her father's already paid the price.'

*   *   *

'There's one thing I don't understand,' I said to Dad, when we were talking about it later. 'If Murphy didn't do it, how did he get involved in all of it – was he set up by Benson or just unlucky?'

'I think he was just in the wrong place at the wrong time,' Dad explained. 'He was wanted by the police anyway, for burglary and theft. He was beginning to annoy them and they thought they'd get him for the murder. Remember that the police were under an awful lot of pressure from the families and the public to find the murderer.'

'There's another thing I don't understand,' I went on.

'What's that?' replied Dad.

'How on earth did you manage to knock Brenda Lovat out with that crazy boxing punch?' I asked. Dad laughed.

'Superior technique, my child,' he said, in his wise parent voice.

I kissed him on his forehead and thought how grateful I was that he was there, that he had always been there.

Chapter 17 *Official pardon*

'Jensen!' Dave Balzano shouted through the open door of his office. I looked at Rick and raised my eyebrows.

'Oh dear,' I said, 'Sounds like our dear editor is in a bad mood.'

It was a couple of months after the Lovat-Murphy case had ended. I had just written my story on it and was waiting for Balzano's judgement. Always a difficult time.

I left my computer and walked nervously over to Balzano's office. If I was going to be in trouble, I might as well go and find out what it was. As usual the few steps over to his office seemed like three kilometres.

'Come in and shut the door, Jensen,' he said as I approached. This was even worse than I had thought. Perhaps I was going to lose my job. With Balzano you could never tell.

I sat down opposite Balzano and waited for the worst. He leant over the desk until his huge face was close to mine. He was sweating and I could see little drops of sweat running down his cheeks.

'Jensen, this story,' he said, waving my story at me.

'Yes,' I said. 'You don't like it . . .?'

'Like it!' he screamed. 'I think it's great. A very good piece of journalism, Jensen. I want it on the front page!!'

'Oh. Well . . . good. I'm glad you like it . . . wonderful

... er.' For once I was lost for words. Balzano never failed to surprise me.

I took the article and went back to my desk. I smiled at Rick to let him know that everything was fine. I allowed myself to read my story one more time before it appeared on the front page of The Daily Echo with my name on it.

Official Pardon for Brendan Murphy
by Kate Jensen

It is over thirty years since Brendan Murphy was hanged for the killing of John Blakeston in the London Road murder, a crime he never committed.

Yesterday Murphy was given a posthumous official pardon by the Home Secretary. The pardon comes after years of campaigning by members of his family and others, a campaign which has been supported by The Daily Echo throughout the long, sad history of this case.

Tony Jensen, the retired journalist who was involved in the reporting of the 1960 murder case and an ex-Echo reporter, led a team of researchers who finally managed to produce new evidence in the case. This new evidence comes from Manchester, where Brendan Murphy was at the time when the murder took place, selling stolen jewellery. Although this alibi came up after the hanging, defence lawyers were never able to prove it without doubt. Now, thirty-five years after Murphy was hanged, witnesses have agreed to swear to Murphy's presence in Manchester, on condition that they will not be prosecuted for crimes committed in the past.

Brenda Lovat-Murphy who is serving a sentence in Durham Prison for murders connected with the clearing of her father's name, said she was delighted at the official pardon. 'This is the happiest day of my life,' she said, 'It's what I've wanted passionately since I first realised that my father was innocent.'

Lovat-Murphy is to be released from prison next year following a further campaign by civil rights campaigners and by this newspaper. Many people, including prison psychologists, believe that Lovat-Murphy will not commit further crimes now that her father has been pardoned. The murders she committed were entirely the result of her father's wrongful hanging.

It will probably never be proved who the London Road murderer really was. Peter Benson, who confessed to the crime after Murphy was hanged, died in 1993.

Yes, it wasn't bad, I thought. Then I thought about Dad, about how proud he was going to be that I would have my story on the front page. I sighed, sat back and smiled to myself, enjoying the moment. Suddenly I heard:

'Jensen!!!! Stop sitting around. I've got another job for you!'